WONDER WI

WE ARE
GREATLY
AMUSED!

WONDER WIMBIN

Everyday Stories of Feminist Folk

CATH JACKSON

Battle Axe Books

First published in Great Britain in 1984
by Battle Axe Books Ltd.
Jubilee House, Chapel Road, Hounslow, Middx TW3 1TX

Distributed via Wildwood House
Trade Orders to: J.M. Dent and Sons (Distribution) Ltd.
Dunhams Lane, Letchworth, Herts.

ISBN 0 946811 01 6

Printed in the U.K.

The Nurse Nightshade cartoons are reproduced by kind permission of Nursing Times

Special thanks to the Trouble and Strife collective, Women's Aid, NALGO, NCCL, City Limits and all the other groups and organisations in whose publications many of these cartoons have appeared.

To all
my friends and
relations, without
whom I would not
be possible.

Cath Jackson was born in Aldershot in 1957. She spent the first twelve years of her life travelling the world with Her Majesty's Armed Forces and the following five at a girls' boarding school in Wiltshire, where she learnt some astonishing Facts of Life and how to play lacrosse. She worked as a very temporary secretary, studied English at university and moved to London in 1980 to become a roving reporter on a construction and civil engineering magazine. Other jobs include printer and publisher, disbudder of carnations and promoter of positive images of lesbians to the largely uncaring world. She now works as a freelance cartoonist and lives in North London with someone else's cat and plants. Her hobbies and interests are many and varied.

40
MILLION
BIGOTS
CAN'T
BE
WRONG!

POEM
ON
CONFLICT
by
Ceres
Amazonchild
Should
i fight the
Man I love
upon the Barricades
es
?

Or should i STAND

and DIE BEside

him

him

TRYING

TO explain ?

JANET GETS IN TOUCH WITH HER NATURAL BODILY RHYTHMS

SANI-PAD
TAMPONS

Z Z Z Z Z

JUST OFF TO MY SELF-DEFENCE CLASS, DEAR

AMBERGRIS, BIRTHWORT, HENBANE...

SQUAW-WEED, BLOOD ROOT, WITCH HAZEL, CHAMOMILE...

...POOR CERES- SHE CAN'T BE WELL...

OR P'RAPS SHE'S TRYING TO CURE HER HOMOEOPATHY?

WOMEN'S REVOLUTION ISN'T ABOUT VIOLENCE...

...MASS UPRISINGS, GUERILLA WARFARE, FIGHTING ON THE STREETS.

IT'S A SLOW AWAKENING, A NEW AWARENESS, A VOICE OF PROTEST FROM THE DEPTHS OF OUR BEINGS

WOMEN THE CULTURAL BARRICADES, SISTERS!

THERE ARE TIMES WHEN REVOLUTIONARY POLITICS SEEM REALLY ATTRACTIVE..

DYING FOR THE CAUSE ON THE BARRICADES.

THE LIFE OF A RADICAL FEMINIST CAN SOMETIMES FEEL

LIKE A TERRIBLE LINGERING WAY TO GO.

WOMBIN!
YOUR LOCAL
WHOLE WOMAN
CENTRE
is NOW
OPEN(ISH)
welcome women!
PLEASE MIND THE 4 FLIGHTS OF STAIRS, FALLING MASONRY AND COUNCIL BAILIFFS!!
HAVE YOU BROUGHT YOUR EARLY MORNING SPECIMEN?
FREE PREGNANCY TESTING
RECLAIM THE DAWN!

DAY CLASSES
MON: RECLAIMING OUR PSYCHIC AWARENESS WITH SKY WATERDAUGHTER
TUES: CERVIX-GAZING WITH IVA SPECULA.
WED: WEAVING AND SPINNING WITH ARIADNE WEBSTER
...AT THE WOMENS CENTRE
WE RUN A LOT OF WOMEN'S ACTIVITIES
IN THERE THEY'RE DOING SELF DEFENCE
TAKE UP A ROCK-LIKE STANCE, GALS
...SHOUT!...
HAH!
...NOW GO FOR HIS GOOLIES!
SHRIEK!
OH LOOK! — IT'S THAT NICE FIRE INSPECTION OFFICER AGAIN!

GAWD! IT'S GOT JANET!
BLEEP BLURP BLOOP!

THERAPY!

WE MUST UNITE TO FIGHT THE LATEST GREATEST THREAT TO FEMINISM AS WE KNOW IT TODAY!!

WE MUST CONFRONT THE ISSUE!
WRITE A PAPER!
CALL A MEETING!
DIARY
LAUNCH A CAMPAIGN!
RAISE THE TITANIC!
AND I...
CONVENE A CONFERENCE
LEAD A WORKSHOP!

MUST GET IN TOUCH WITH MY FATIGUE

EXCUSE ME-
DO YOU SPEAK
ENGELISH?

THE WHOLE-WOMBAN CENTRE
All Wimmin Welcome!
DING DONG

I'LL JUST CALL THE **LIFT**
FLICK!

Hi!
Hi

ONLY ANOTHER FIVE FLIGHTS TO GO!!
DARE I ASK FOR THE LOO?

IN THERAPY
GLOOOOOOM

MY GOD! THERE'S **CAT SHIT** UNDER MY CHAIR.

IF I SAY SOMETHING SHE'LL THINK I'M **ANALLY OBSESSED**.

AND IF I **DON'T** SAY SOMETHING SHE'LL **KNOW** I'M THINKING WHAT I'M THINKING AND SHE'LL THINK I'M TRYING TO **HIDE** MY **ANALITY...**

YOUR CAT'S SHAT UNDER MY CHAIR!
WHAT MAKES YOU THINK I **HAVE** A CAT?

Celebrate the Body Beautiful.

Sing the Songs of Creation.

Dance to the Moon and Mother Earth.

Peace!

Fecundity! Serenity!

Teabreak

AND WHAT ARE **WE** KNITTING TODAY?
BALACLAVAS FOR THE ANGRY BRIGADE.

AT THE WOMEN'S CENTRE
LETTERS
THE CENTRE IS USED BY A LOT OF WOMEN'S GROUPS.
BLACK WOMENS GROUP
WORKING CLASS WOMENS GROUP
LESBIAN WOMEN'S GROUP
OLDER WOMENS GROUP
AND LOTS MORE!
ACTUALLY THEY'RE ALL ON HOLIDAY IN CRETE AT THE MOMENT—EXCEPT THIS LOT...
THE GUILT-RIDDEN WOMEN'S GROUP.

AT THE WOMEN'S CENTRE
DEEP IN THE BOWELS OF THE BASEMENT THE SISTERSEZ NEWSLETTER COLLECTIVE DISCUSSES A CONTRIBUTION OF DUBIOUS POLITICAL PURITY...
WELL—IT DOESN'T CONTRAVENE THE SEVEN DEMANDS...
IT'S NOT SEXIST OR RACIST...
OR CLASSIST OR AGEIST...
BUT IT'S NOT ON A STENCIL...
AND IT'S NOT SIGNED...
ANYONE SEEN MY SHOPPING LIST?
—MUST HAVE GOT INTO THE WRONG PIGEON-HOLE...

DRIVEL..DRONE...
BLAH...
POINT OF ORDER, COMRADE BROTHER CHAIRMAN-PERSON.
IT'S YOUR TURN TO BABYSIT...
AND SHE'S JUST PASSED A MOTION OF NO CONFIDENCE.

MEN OUT!
MEN OUT!
GET 'EM OUT!
SISTERS! SISTERS!
NO MEN

I KNOW WE DON'T WANT MEN AT OUR MEETINGS ··· BUT THESE GUYS ARE OUR BROTHERS...

THEY WANT TO HELP! THEY CAN BE USEFUL TO US··· AND ANYWAY...

IT'S THEIR HALL.

SISTERS! SISTERS! WHERE'S THE SENSE IN SEPARATISM?

BETTER TO WORK WITH MEN THAN TO LET THEM DIVIDE US.

IF WE STAND ALONE WE STAND TO LOSE...

MY LABOUR PARTY MEMBERSHIP.
WITH THANKS TO SOPHIE

BE Y A Y FRONT?

RIDE ON, SISTER-
RIDE ON...!

FRANK AND I ARE GOING TO THE PEACE CAMP.

I'M GOING TO PICKET AND FRANK'S GOING TO MAKE SANDWICHES IN SUPPORT.

FRANK SAYS IT'S REALLY IMPORTANT FOR WOMEN TO ORGAN-ISE AUTONOMOUSLY.

BUT HE WANTS TO BE AROUND IN CASE THERE'S ANY TROUBLE.

JUST FINISH FRANK'S SARNIES- THEN I MUST GO AND PACK FOR THE PEACE CAMP.

KAOLIN AND MORPHINE, PLASTIC SHEETING... JUST A FEW ESSENTIALS

FRANK THINKS I SHOULD TAKE SOME-THING SYMBOLIC TO HANG ON THE FENCE

HOW ABOUT FRANK?

Introducing Vera...

O CLITORIA, HOW I ADORE YA!
SOME SAY IT ALL BEGAN WITH SAPPHO, PENNING LINES OF LOVE TO HER GOLDEN GIRL.

OTHERS PREFER TO LOOK TO HUMBLER, THO' NO LESS SIG-NIFICANT, ANTECEDENTS...

AND CULTURE...
JEN FOR SUZI
PENNY JANET
TINA IS A RIGHT-ON DYKE
KILL MEN
IT'S THE KINDEST WAY
I LOVE BARBRA

OR, FOR THE REAL PURISTS
NEANDERTHAL DYKE WOZ 'ERE!

THE LOVE THAT DARES NOT SPEAK ITS NAME EXPRESSES ITSELF IN MANY OBLIQUE AND CURIOUS WAYS.
VERA

I'M JUST A PHASE YOU'RE GOING THROUGH.
O PASH O CRUSH O P.I.A*!
* PERSON I ADORE

...BUT WHATEVER ITS ORIGINS, WHEN WE LOOK HARD AND CLE-ARLY AT THE EXTENT AND ELAB-ORATION OF MEASURES DESIGNED TO KEEP WOMEN WITHIN A MALE SEXUAL PURLIEU, IT BE-COMES AN INESCAPABLE QUESTION
ISSUE WE HAVE TO
FEMINISTS IS, NOT
INEQUALITY*...
ZZZZZZZ
* A. RICH

LESBIANS IGNITE IN ARMED SNUGGLE

AND STAY AWAY FROM YOUR MUM— I DON'T WANT YOU GIVING HER ANY IDEAS.
3

COMING OUT: A PERSONAL AND PUBLIC DECLARATION OF OUR TRUE SEXUAL SELVES. A SYMBOLIC THROWING OPEN OF THE CLOSET...

I'M A LESBIAN!

LAUNDRY

OR WHATEVER RECEPTACLE IN WHICH WE HAVE BEEN IMMURED BY HETEROSEXIST AND PATRIARCHAL VALUES.

SODOM TODAY... GOMORRAH THE WORLD!

AND ONCE YOU'RE "OUT"...

YOU NEED NEVER FEEL ALONE AGAIN.

PLEASE MISS, WHAT'S A LESBIAN?

LESBIANS COME IN ALL SHAPES AND SIZES...
IN ALL AGES, COLOURS, RACES, CLASSES AND CREEDS.
BUT WE ALL SHARE ONE FOREMOTHER – THE GREATEST LESBIAN OF US ALL...
THE INVISIBLE LESBIAN
DESPISED, DENIED, FORGOTTEN, IGNORED, BELITTLED, BERATED BUT
ALWAYS THERE!
CJ

WE LESBIANS HAVE VARIOUS DISTINCTIVE WAYS OF DRESSING.
WHAT THE WELL-DRESSED DYKE IS WEARING
(clothes designed by Gross Stereotypes Unlimited)
AERTEX
PHEEP!
TRACKSUIT
TRAINERS
SENSIBLE TWEEDS
BRIEFCASE
FLATTIES
PROTECTIVE HAIRCUT
LEATHERS
FADED JEANS
MORE HAND-KNITTING
JUMBLE SALE
GUCCI
HAND-KNIT
CO-OP MADE
CERTAIN ITEMS OF CLOTHING HAVE SPECIAL SIGNIFICANCE... A HANKY IN THE BACK POCKET, FOR EXAMPLE, MEANS – "I'VE GOT A HEAVY COLD"...
WHILE A WINCYETTE NIGHTIE (FLORAL) MEANS – "I'M GOING TO BED...
...ALONE."
© 1985 CATH JACKSON

WE MUST ADDRESS THE ISSUE OF CLASS!

WE MUST ADDRESS THE ISSUE OF RACE!

HEY, SISTER...
TING!

HOW ABOUT ADDRESSING A FEW ENVELOPES.

COOKING FOR FRIENDS IS A REAL PROBLEM WHEN THEY'RE ALL ON DIFFERENT DIETS.
THE ALL-EARTH COOK-BOOK
MS. BEETON
VEGGIE GLUPPS
COOKING FOR CARNIVORES
LIVER SALTS
DODIE IS A VEGAN
Bacon Butty
Pulse, Pulse...
MARGE IS A MACROBIOTIC
AMY'S A GRAMNIVORE
AND I'M A HOMNIVORE!
I EAT MEN!

LESBIANS ARE EMOTIONALLY IMMATURE, SEXUALLY PROMISCUOUS, AND UNABLE TO MAINTAIN STABLE ADULT RELATIONSHIPS.
REPUTABLE STUFFED SHIRT
SEZ YOU

DR. VERA DE VISIBLE B.Sc., Ph.D., M.D., E.T.C., HAS BEEN DOING SOME INDEPENDENT RESEARCH INTO LESBIAN SEXUAL PRACTICES...
DIVORCE RATES
HETS: 1 IN 3
LESBIANS 0 !!

SERIOUSLY THO'— IT'S A MYTH THAT LESBIANS ARE SEXUALLY PROLIFIC...
DISREPUTABLE DYKE

WE JUST SPEND A LOT OF TIME TALKING ABOUT IT.
HEARD ABOUT ANNIE AND JULIA?
WHAT WAS THAT?
—AND JULIA AND ASTRID AND ASTRID AND JO AND
SEX, LUST AND THE POLITICS OF DESIRE!
WITH HER T-SHIRT ON...?!

SPRING
AUTUMN
WINTER
VRoom
BIKE DYKE
Summer
WARRoom
BIKINI DYKINI?

I DON'T CARE IF SHE'S SPENDING THE NIGHT WITH PHYLLIS PHABB LEAD GUITAR WITH THE DYKES DINNER WIMBIN'S ROCK BAND.

I'M NOT INTO MONOGAMY, JEALOUSY, POWER GAMES, --- FIDELITY --- TRUST --- LOVE --- HET. CONCEPTS OF OWNERSHIP...
DOG

I LIKE BEING ALONE

AUGH!

MY HOT WATER BOTTLE'S LEAKING
Oh yeah?

AND I'LL HAVE MY DUSTY SPRINGFIELD L.P.s BACK!
WHEN A RELATIONSHIP FINISHES...

TICK TOCK
IT'S GOOD TO BE CELIBATE FOR A WHILE.

TICK TOCK
TAKE TIME TO THINK, READ, EXPLORE YOURSELF AND LEARN.

TICK TOCK
TWIDDLE

THERE! THAT SHOULD BE LONG ENOUGH!
TICK!

TOWARDS A FEMINIST NEUROTICA

WRITE-OFF
WOMEN'S
BOOKSHOP
HEALTH
TO OURSELVES
BY OURSELVES
WITH OURSELVES
OFF OUR HEADS
SELF-EXAM PAPERS VOL. 1.
OUR OWN SELVES
BEARING OUR LOAD
D.I.Y. BABY BOOK
RECLAIM THE MOON
REGYNERATION
PATRIARCHAL POSTURES
RECLAIM EVERYTHING
POLITICS
HERSTORY
SPINNING OUR OWN THREADS
MATRIARCHY MANUAL
WHO DID WHAT...
...AND WHEN (AUTH. VERSION)

CAN I HELP YOU?
LESBIAN
THE WELL OF LONELINESS
DESERT OF THE HEART
DEPTHS OF DESPAIR
WILDERNESS OF WOE
DYKE'S PROGRESS
PASSIONATE FRIENDS

HAVE YOU GOT 'THE JOY OF LESBIAN SEX'?
TRY UNDER "FICTION".

AT THE COOL COYOTE DISCO...
HI DODIE!
HI VERA!
HERE ON YOUR OWN?
YEAH–JUS' CRUISIN'...
ME TOO– SEEYA 'ROUND.
YEAH– SEEYA...
LATER THAT NIGHT...
NO LUCK?
NOPE.
ME NEITHER
–BEEN TO ANY GOOD MEETINGS LATELY?

THAT'S FUNNY. THE FRIDGE IS FULL OF CHEESE.
JUST OFF DOWN THE SHOPS!
HMMM...
...FOLLOW DAT LADY...
SUPERMARKET
LARV is a many spLENdoured thing...
–JUST AS I SUSPECTED...
QUARTER OF DOLCELATTE PLEASE
MILD CHEDDAR
ANOTHER ONE OF VERA'S IMPOSSIBLE PASSIONS...

NOT TONIGHT SWEETEST – I'VE GOT A GUILT-TRIP COMING ON

YOU BEEN TO · GREENHAM?
YEAH

GOT ARRESTED FOR HANGING NAPPIES ON THE FENCE.

GREAT GESTURE.
YOU THINK SO?

I WAS ONLY TRYING TO DRY THEM.

VERA AND HER MEDIA WATCH WOMEN'S GROUP ARE DOING SOME IMPORTANT RESEACH. SUDDENLY...
OOOH! THAT ELSIE TANNER!
R.I.P
BOING
AW, BABS!
I CAN'T SEE THE TELLY...
ZOOOM!
SPOILSPORT
KISS KISS
CHERISH CHERISH
NOURISH
NURTURE
LOVE
YUM!
I THINK SHE WAS GETTING IN TOUCH WITH HER BODY...
WHAT WAS THAT ABOUT?
COULDN'T SHE DO IT BY LETTER?
MEANWHILE, BACK AT THE ROVERS RETURN...

WELL... IT'S THE SPECIAL NON-BREATHING NIGHT AT THE PIED COW CELLAR — THAT'S A WOMEN-ONLY DISCO...
RING RING!
HELLO? LESBIAN SWITCHBOARD!
WHERE DID I GO WRONG?
LOOK, MOTHER...
YOU MUST STOP RINGING ME AT WORK.
P'RAPS YOU SHOULD STAY IN AND WATCH DALLAS...

LESBIAN WHEN YOU WERE THREE? THAT'S NOTHING. I HAD A CRUSH ON THE MID-WIFE.

IT'S CHRISTMAS EVE AND VERA IS PUTTING GILLY AND SAMANTHA TO BED.
IS, IS!
ISN'T, ISN'T!
I'M AN AID BABY

GILLY SAYS FATHER CHRISTMAS DOESN'T EXIST!
OF COURSE HE DOESN'T

BUT THERE IS A SISTERS OF SOLSTICE COLLECTIVE – AND THEY'RE PROBABLY ON THE ROOF NOW, WAITING FOR YOU TO GO TO SLEEP SO THEY CAN BRING YOU YOUR PRESENTS...

O.K. — SO WHERE IS EVERYONE?
WELL, SUE'S GONE HOME TO HER MUM'S, DILL'S SEEING HER THERAPIST, ANN'S AT GREENHAM, JULIE'S WITH HER LOVER, JO'S AT HER SELF-INSEMINATION GROUP...
WHATEVER HAPPENED TO POLITICAL PURITY?

PROFESSOR IGOR GETOFFONIT WOULD LIKE TO KNOW WHAT LESBIANS DO IN BED.

SO HERE ARE A FEW FANCIFUL SUGGESTIONS...
COUNTING SHEEP IS A GOOD WAY TO PASS TIME...
AM I A LESBIAN SHEEP BECAUSE I AM COUNTED BY A LESBIAN?
THO' COUNTING LESBIANS IS MORE FUN!
3 TRILLION BILLION MILLION... AND I'M SURE ANGIE'S ON THE TURN...

SOME MAKE REVOLUTION
AND NOW FOR THE SUPREME POLITICAL ACT!
WHICH PAGE IS SHE ON...?
THE JOY OF LESBIAN SEX

MOSTLY WE MAKE CRUMBS
I'M IN LOVE WITH A CHOC-CHIP COOKIE

ON READING FREUD

LET US TAKE A STROLL DOWN THE LESBIAN LITERATI HALL OF FAME.

VIRGINIA "WAS-SHE-WASN'T-SHE" WOOLF — NOVELIST AND FAMOUS PROFILE ...

ALICE B. TOKLAS - ONLY WOMAN TO HAVE A BIT-PART IN HER OWN AUTOBIOGRAPHY.
I DENY IT!
K. MANSFIELD

AND LAST, BUT BY NO MEANS LEAST ... THE WELL ITSELF.
IT'S SO LONESOME ON YOUR OWNSOME
DO NOT TOUCH

GREEK FLOWER, GREEK ECSTACY! RECLAIMS FOR EVER ONE WHO DIED FOLLOWING INTRICATE SONG'S LAST MEASURE.
(H.D.)
(1886-1961)

I LOVE WOMEN'S POETRY — THE ANCIENT RHYMES OF SAPPHO, H.D.'S CHEERY EPITAPHS — EVEN SOME OF TODAY'S TACKY NUMBERS ABOUT THE QUINTESSENTIAL JOYS OF MOTHERHOOD
NAPPY RASH
OR
POETRY IN MOTIONS
A VERSE CHRONICLE OF BABYS BOWELS
BY
A Non biological mother

OUR FORESISTERS OF THE EARLY 1900'S ARE GREAT — WRITING CLOSET POMES ABOUT THEIR LESBIAN LOVERS ...
THEY'RE MOSTLY DEAD NOW, BUT THEY STILL HAVE POWER TO SHAKE THE LITERARY ESTABLISHMENTS ...
← YES, LESBIANS DO THEIR IRONING TOO.
IN THIS SHORT SONNET THE LITTLE-KNOWN POET, D.L., LAMENTS THE DEATH OF HER LOVER ...

AS THEY TURN IN THEIR GRAVES.
HISS!
ONE OF THE MILLIONS OF FINE YOUNG MEN SLAIN IN THEIR PRIME IN THE FIRST WORLD WAR.
COPYRIGHT © 1983 CATH JACKSON

YOU MOVED!

VERA AND HER GOOD FRIEND BIJOU JOHNETTE ARE ON THEIR WAY TO LITTLE-HENNINGTON-IN-THE-WOLD, HOPING TO LEARN MORE ABOUT THE GREAT LESBIAN POET, D.L.…
THE SAPPHO ARMS
SNUG
HO! THIS LOOKS PROMISING. LET'S STOP FOR LUNCH.
TWO CHEESE PLOUGHMANS AND TWO PINTS, PLEASE.
-SORRY DEAR-
WE ONLY DO SHERRY AND CUCUMBER SANDWICHES.

NOW ON TO "LITTLE LESBOS" TO VISIT THE MISSES LETTICE AND FENELLA DIBLEY, CLOSE FRIENDS OF D.L.
PARP! PARP!
MISS DIBLEY? I'M VERA- AND THIS IS MY ASSISTANT, BIJOU JOHNETTE
HMPH! GOT A MAN WITH YOU THEN?
ER… YES… BUT HE'S A MAN AGAINST SEXISM!
AND WHAT EXACTLY DOES THAT MEAN?
I OFTEN WONDER…
COPYRIGHT © 1983 CATH JACKSON

And to my dear husband I bequeath my lack of pension rights.

I'M THINKING OF GETTING HIM DONE SOON

BONG
BONG
BONG
BONG
BONG
BONG
WELL DEARS, YOU MUST GO NOW. WE HAVE ANOTHER MEETING THIS EVENING.

"POETRY READINGS AND REMINISCENCES" AT THE VILLAGE HALL — THEY TOLD US ABOUT IT AT THE PUB.

GRACIOUS NO, DEARIE, THAT'S JUST FOR THE TOURISTS...
SAPPHIC DILLY-DO'S ON THE WOLD...? LESSY TUPPER-WARE PARTIES? JAM-MAKING FOR THE ISOLATED LESBIAN?

WE'RE OFF TO THE MONTHLY HENNINGTON DIESEL-DYKE CONVENTION!!

HERE WE GO AGAIN...
FIGHT!

NNNG!
AUGH!
ERRG!

WHAT A WASTE!

THOSE POOR LITTLE EGGS··· ALL THAT GOOD RED BLOOD··· ALL THAT FECUNDITY···

VERA! I'VE DECIDED!

WE'RE GOING TO HAVE A BABY!
"WE"?

VERA HAS JUST LEARNED SHE IS TO BE A NON-BIOLOGICAL MOTHER
APOCALYPTIC VISION OF NEXT SISTER SHACK LESBIAN HOUSING CO-OP MEETING···
BUT WHY?
BUT WHEN?
BUT HOW?
'COURSE NOT, SILLY···
NOT... NOT... NOT WITH A MAN?!?

ALL I NEED IS A NICE CLEAN JAM-JAR···
PERSEPHONE'S ORGANIC POMEGRANITE PRESERVE

GRANNY'S BASTER···

...AND A NICE CLEAN, GUARANTEED ANTI-SEXIST, SUPER-FERTILE SPERM DONOR.
ADDRESS BOOK

HOW ABOUT YOUR EX-HUSBAND?
I'LL FORGET YOU SAID THAT···

ANTI-SEXIST MEN DO THE HOOVERING —

CHANGE THE BABY'S NAPPY (SOMETIMES) —

HELP WITH THE WASHING-UP —

AND PUT THEIR WHOLE-HEARTED SUPPORT AT THE FRONT OF WOMEN'S POLITICAL STRUGGLE.

ABBY HAS JOINED A LESBIAN SELF-INSEMINATION GROUP.

HOW DID YOUR D.I.Y. MEETING GO, THEN?

SSH! I'M PRACTISING CREATING A WELCOMING ENVIRONMENT FOR GYNOSPERM.

NO CHIPS FOR ME, LOVE! I'M ON A SPECIAL GRAPEFRUIT AND YOGHURT DIET.

BUT GRAPEFRUIT GIVES YOU MIGRAINE

SALT

MALT VINEGAR

DR. WENDY WELL-WOMBYN WRITES: The male androsperm is much weaker than the female gynosperm and does not like an acid environment. Our sister gynosperm, however, flourishes in these circumstances and will easily beat the weakened male in the life and death race to fertilise the egg.

AH! TIME FOR MY VAGINAL DOUCHE

'ERE! COME BACK WITH THE VINEGAR!

SOME OF US ARE GOING TO HAVE TO LEARN TO MAKE A FEW SACRIFICES...

SALT

CONTINUING THE SAGA OF ABBY'S A.I.D. ADVENTURES...

I MUST BE CRAZY! — HANGING ROUND KINGS CROSS, WAITING TO PICK UP A JAR OF SPERM FROM SOME ANONYMOUS GAY GUY...

LEFT LUGGAGE

OH-OH! I RECOGNISE THAT WALK!

BIJOU! HOW COME YOU'RE INVOLVED IN THIS?

I'M GIVING UP MY ULTIMATE PATRIARCHAL PRIVILEGES!!

I SMELL A BIJOU PLOTETTE

© BIJOU PRODUCTS INC.

KINDLY SEXUALLY ORIENTATE YOURSELF ELSEWHERE.

Dear Mother,
Guess what?! I've decided to HAVE A BABY!!

I know you will want to share this wonderful experience with me. I want you to be involved too. I feel it's really im-portant to reclaim our ancient trad-itions of mother daughter bonding.
your loving daughter
Abby x

Dear daughter,
Nuts! You're mad! Have sold your father and am going on a world cruise.
yr mum
Mum
xx

Mum
xx
P.S. Why can't you use the telephone like every-one else? This is the 20th century you know.

!

HELLO MOM? CAN I COME TOO?

KITTI BOX

...MAKE SAND-WICHES FOR THEIR LUNCHES, SEE KIDS OFF TO SCHOOL, SEE HUSBAND OFF TO WORK, WASH UP, MAKE-UP, GET DRESSED, FEED AND DRESS BABY, CLEAN UP BABY-SICK, TAKE BABY TO CHILDMINDER–

...MISS BUS, WALK TO WORK. ARRIVE AT NINE.

TWO O'CLOCK – A (LATE) LUNCH-BREAK...

BACK TO WORK. MISS UNION MEETING. MISS LAST POST. LEAVE LATE...
HUH! WOMEN DON'T CARE ABOUT POLITICS...
TAKE TWENTY LETTERS, MRS. BROWN.

COLLECT BABY, GET HOME, GREET KIDS, POP IN ON ELDERLY NEIGHBOUR, GREET HUSBAND.
LATE AGAIN MRS. B...
SORRY...

COOK SUPPER....
C'MON WOMAN! I'LL BE LATE DOWN THE PUB!

TICK TOCK
WASH UP. BATH BABY. PUT KIDS TO BED.
TICK TOCK
DO LAUNDRY. PUT HUSBAND TO BED. CLEAN HOUSE.
TICK TOCK
IRON WASHING. MEND SOCKS.
PUT OUT DUSTBINS. PREPARE BREAKFAST THINGS. GET UP AT SEVEN...
BRRING!
NO-THAT'S NOT RIGHT... I HAVEN'T BEEN TO BED YET...
THANK-YOU, MRS. BROWN!
WHAT A BUSY LIFE! A BIG HAND, LADIES AND GENTS, FOR THE...ER...
CLUNK
LATE MRS. BROWN!
CLAP CLAP!

WHEEEEEEE!!!
NEAT, EH?

NURSE NIGHTSHADE

I FEEL OPPRESSED

HMMPH! THEY'VE CUT MEALS ON WHEELS AGAIN.

NOW NURSE!

MOST DOCTORS DON'T SMOKE!

YEAH

AND NONE OF 'EM NURSE.

WHEN I DIE...

I'M LEAVING MY BODY TO MEDICAL SCIENCE.

I ALREADY DID.

BUT I'M STILL IN IT.

WELL–YOU SAID TO PUT IT IN WRITING
GIMME MY RIGHTS
D.H.S.S.

"A YOUNG GIRL IS BROUGHT IN COMPLAINING OF SEVERE ABDOMINAL PAINS.
A URINE TEST SHOWS 2% GLUCOSE AND KETONES.

zZZ
Grrr

SISTER!

STAFF!

NURSE!

BED PAN

PATIENTS! PATIENTS! AAAGH!!

WHAT YOU NEED, ENID...

IS NURSE NIGHTSHADE'S CURE-ALL FOR DIFFICULT CASES.

GROUND GLASS.

WORTS FOR WOMEN
FREE HERBS ON DEMAND
GOD'S BONES- 'TIS THE RADICAL WITCHES GROUP

REVENGE OF THE INVISIBLE WOMAN

OW!

TWEAK!

CLANG

WHO DID THIS TO YOU?

IT WAS... IT WAS...

Tee Hee!

A NURSE!

ACTUALLY I WAS HOPING FOR SOMETHING A LITTLE MORE MODERN
HOUSING DEPT.

NURSE NIGHTSHADE

AND THE CLINICAL STUDENT

SWABS, NURSE.

SAY PLEASE

PLEASE

IT MAKES A NICE CHANGE FROM POT PLANTS

NURSE NIGHTSHADE
NEXT OF KIN?
ANN GREEN
SHE'S MY LOVER, ACTUALLY.
WHAT DID I SAY?
ISOLATION WARD
KEEP OUT
CJ

IN

OUT

PENDING

YOU MEAN THERE'S NOTHING IN THIS FEMINISM FOR ME?
BAH! THAT'S NOT DEMOCRATIC.

POSITIVE ACTION PROGRAMME

MAKE US A CUP OF TEA, LOVE.
BAN THE BOMB
CND RALLY
JOBS NOT BOMBS

TAP! TAP
TAPPETY-TAP
TAP TAP
TAP
TAP
TAP
TAP!
TIP TAP
TIPPETY TAP
TIP TAP

TAP TAP TAP—
TAPPETY-TAPPETY
TiP TAP TAP
THUNK!
TAP TAP
TAP TAP
TAP TAP
TAP...

CHANGING ROOMS
IT DOESN'T FIT...

'S VALENTINE'S DAY—
COCK-A DOODLE-DOOO

A SPECIAL DAY IN EVERY GIRL'S LIFE!
SNARL

SHE WAKES BRIGHT AND EARLY...
BLEAGH!

IN ORDER TO PERFORM THE COMPLEX RITUALS...
SCRATCH
YAWN
STRETCH
TWIDDLE

I'M NOT WELL
HICH WILL ENSURE...

I SHOULD BE IN BED
THAT WHEN SHE FIRST LOOKS IN THE MIRROR...

AWK!
SHE WILL SEE, REFLECTED BEHIND HER,...

THAT'S NEVER ANOTHER SPOT ON MY NOSE!?
THE FACE OF THE LOVED ONE SHE IS TO WED.

1987
1986
1985
1984
1983
1982
1981
1980
1979
0
1
2
3
4
5
6
7
8
DID SHE FALL...
OR WAS SHE
NATURALLY WASTED?
(MILLIONS)
UNEMPLOYMENT

M.D.

COMPLETE WORKS of ENGELS
PLINK!

S
UM